Did You
DURHAM
A MISCELLANY

Compiled by Julia Skinner

With particular reference to the work of Derek Mackenzie-Hook

THE FRANCIS FRITH COLLECTION

www.francisfrith.com

Based on a book first published in the United Kingdom in 2006 by The Francis Frith Collection®

This edition published exclusively for Identity Books in 2009 ISBN 978-1-84589-393-4

Text and Design copyright The Francis Frith Collection®
Photographs copyright The Francis Frith Collection® except where indicated.

The Frith® photographs and the Frith® logo are reproduced under licence from
Heritage Photographic Resources Ltd, the owners of the Frith® archive and trademarks.
'The Francis Frith Collection', 'Francis Frith' and 'Frith' are registered trademarks of
Heritage Photographic Resources Ltd.

British Library Cataloguing in Publication Data

Did You Know? Durham - A Miscellany
Compiled by Julia Skinner
With particular reference to the work of Derek Mackenzie-Hook

The Francis Frith Collection
Frith's Barn, Teffont,
Salisbury, Wiltshire SP3 5QP
Tel: +44 (0) 1722 716 376
Email: info@francisfrith.co.uk
www.francisfrith.com

Printed and bound in Singapore

Front Cover: **DURHAM, THE COUNT'S HOUSE 1914** 67129p

The colour-tinting is for illustrative purposes only, and is not intended to be historically accurate

AS WITH ANY HISTORICAL DATABASE, THE FRANCIS FRITH ARCHIVE IS CONSTANTLY BEING
CORRECTED AND IMPROVED, AND THE PUBLISHERS WOULD WELCOME INFORMATION ON
OMISSIONS OR INACCURACIES

CONTENTS

Did You Know?
DURHAM
A MISCELLANY

INTRODUCTION

Durham is a beautiful city that is both fascinating and interesting in a myriad ways. Its cathedral, castle, university, ancient schools, bridges, churches, market place and array of public buildings are the principal threads woven into the colourful tapestry which is the city today. It is regarded as the historic capital of north-east England, as an important centre for culture and learning, and not least as an area of great natural beauty. The historic significance of Durham is inexorably linked with its being regarded as one of the cradles of Christianity in England. It was the final resting-place of St Cuthbert, who died in AD687, and whose remains were brought here in AD995. The magnificent cathedral remains the city's chief glory. Durham's special qualities were officially recognised by UNESCO in 1986 when its cathedral and castle were included in the first selection of World Heritage Sites, along with other universally known places such as Stonehenge and the Taj Mahal.

The site for Durham was probably originally chosen for its good defensive position, and the area has seen its share of conflict over the centuries, although the castle proved to be the only northern castle never to fall to the Scots. It was not until the 18th and 19th centuries that the declining threat of constant invasion meant that life in Durham could change. This newfound stability prompted redevelopment on a scale not seen in the city for hundreds of years. Durham began to assume its modern character, and grand country and town houses were built for the landed gentry, the lawyers and the merchants. Many had prospered from exploiting coalfields beneath their land, but fortunately for Durham the seams beneath the city were not worth mining - otherwise many of the historic buildings could have been affected by subsidence.

Many of the older buildings associated with the city's industrial development have now been demolished, and the increase in population has seen the modern city expand outwards - Durham now has a population of about 80,000 compared with about 2,000 in 1635. However, the completion of the new inner through road in the early 1970s means that vehicles moving across the city can now avoid passing through the market place, taking some of the traffic pressure from the historic city core. The vibrant city of modern Durham still has a remarkable variety of streets and buildings of all ages and has managed to retain much of its original character. Even today, a 14th-century monk would have little difficulty in recognising some of the buildings portrayed in the photographs included in this book.

The story of Durham is full of fascinating characters and events, of which this book can only provide a brief glimpse.

PREBENDS' BRIDGE AND THE RIVER BANK 1914 67132

COUNTY DURHAM WORDS AND PHRASES

'Ahint' - behind.

'Badly liked' - disliked.

'Bairn' - small child. *'Grand-bairns'* - grandchildren.

'Bank' - hill.

'Beck' or *'burn'* - a stream.

'Butterloggy' or *'butterlowey'* - a butterfly.

'Chancetimes' - occasionally.

'Chimla' - chimney.

'Dickyhedgie' - a hedge-sparrow.

'Ha' waxed folk' - children.

'Hand's turn' - a stroke of work.

'Mackem' - a person from Sunderland.

'Skelp' - smack.

'Throng' - busy, very crowded, as in *'It were throng in there!'*

'Tidy Betty' - a bottomless fender across the fire grate.

'Whisht!' - Hush, be quiet!

'Wishful' - desirous, wanting something.

HAUNTED DURHAM

The former Grammar School building on Palace Green is said to be haunted by the ghost of a young pupil who was thrown from a balcony by one of his masters in a fit of anger.

In medieval times a number of structures were built on Elvet Bridge, including the chapels of St Andrew and St James which stood at either end. The latter was replaced by the House of Correction in 1632; this was the former home of Jamie Allan, a celebrated Northumbrian piper and sometime villain. It is said that the strains of Allan's pipes are still to be heard around Elvet Bridge.

A former cell on the ground floor of Durham prison is said to be haunted by the ghost of a prisoner who was murdered there with a kitchen knife by another inmate in 1947. Other prisoners who were kept in the cell after the murder complained of seeing ghostly re-enactments of the event during the night, and the cell was converted into a storeroom.

Crook Hall, by the River Wear to the north of Durham, is said to be haunted by a White Lady who on St Thomas's Eve (20 December) glides down the blocked-off staircase which links the older, medieval part of the Hall with the later Jacobean sections. There have been several reported sightings of the ghost, which is sometimes accompanied by a rustling sound, as of a silk dress. In 1989 a previous owner, Mary Hawgood, said that she woke in the middle of the night whilst sleeping in the Medieval Bedroom and saw the White Lady, who she described as 'wearing a long dress, and I saw her outlined as she was bathed in a pool of light, or rather was outlined against it'. The present owners, Keith and Maggie Bell, have also reported hearing strange noises, including the sound of footsteps ascending the staircase - and going on into what is now an empty space.

Crossgate Peth is associated with two ghosts. One is that of a woman carrying a baby, thought to be the wife of a soldier who was killed at the Battle of Neville's Cross in the Middle Ages; the other is also a woman, this time without a child, said to be the shade of a young woman who was murdered in the 19th century.

The building known as the Grey Tower in North Road is said to be haunted - a ghostly face sometimes appears at an attic window.

DURHAM MISCELLANY

Durham was once in the powerful Anglo-Saxon kingdom of Northumbria, which became one of the great centres of early Christianity following the conversion of King Oswald; it was he who founded the monastery on the island of Lindisfarne in AD635. The devout and respected Cuthbert was ordained Bishop of Lindisfarne in AD685, but ill health forced him to resign his see and he died on Farne Island in AD687. He was buried at Lindisfarne, and his tomb quickly became a place of pilgrimage. So many miracles were reported at his grave that Cuthbert was called 'the wonder-worker of England', and was canonised eleven years after his death. In AD875 the Community of St Cuthbert finally abandoned Lindisfarne to the invading Vikings; carrying the saint's bones with them, they sought sanctuary elsewhere. After several years of wandering around Northumbria the Community settled at Chester-le-Street in AD883, and St Cuthbert was laid to rest in the Saxon church there; however, in AD995, with the threat of further Viking raids looming, the Community were once more on the move. It is said that the saint himself intervened in the selection of Durham as a permanent resting place (see page 9), but the defensive qualities of a peninsula with high steep banks and almost completely surrounded by water would not have been lost on the monks.

The great round-headed doorway shown in photograph 30762, opposite, was once the principal entrance to the lower part of the 12th-century building that stands directly opposite the gatehouse of Durham Castle. It was probably approached under a canopy by a long flight of steps from the courtyard. The doorway is in near immaculate condition, and is believed by many to be one of the finest examples of late Romanesque stone carving in England.

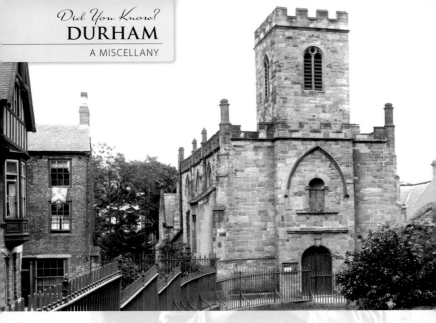

THE CHURCH OF ST MARY-LE-BOW 1918 68230

The Church of St Mary-le-Bow is thought to occupy the site of
the first Saxon church to be built on the peninsula, which was
where St Cuthbert's remains were housed when they were first
brought to Durham. The sacred relics first rested in a hastily
erected church built from boughs of trees and roofed with
turf (the Church of Boughs). The medieval church of St Mary-
le-Bow was rebuilt in 1683, and the tower was added in 1703.
St Mary-le-Bow was the parish church for the northern part of
the peninsula (see photograph 68230, above). The church is
now a Heritage Centre, telling the story of the city of Durham
from medieval times to the present day.

Legend says that after years of wandering the north, the guardians of St Cuthbert's coffin came to a halt at a hill called Warden Law. Despite all the efforts of the monks, the cart carrying the coffin would not move any further, so their leader committed them to three days of fasting and prayer in order to learn the reason why the coffin would not move. Their prayers were finally answered when St Cuthbert appeared in a dream to a monk called Eadmer, and told him that the coffin should be taken to a place called Dun Holm. ('Dun' was an Anglo-Saxon word deriving from Celtic meaning 'hill', and 'holm', meaning 'island', is a word of Scandinavian origin.) The monks discovered that they were now able to move the coffin and set off in search of the hill on an island. On their way they overheard a conversation between two milkmaids who were also on their way to Dun Holm to search for a lost cow, so they decided to follow them, and eventually reached their destination. Once the monks arrived on Dun Holm's rocky peninsula, they instantly decided that this would be an appropriate place for St Cuthbert's shrine. Over the years the name has been simplified to the modern form - Durham.

When the remains of St Cuthbert were first brought to Durham they were housed in a temporary church (see opposite). The monks of the Community of St Cuthbert later built a more substantial white-washed timber building, called the White Church, which was eventually replaced in AD999 by the Anglo-Saxon minster, built of stone and also white-washed. This white church soon became a place of pilgrimages as miracles attributed to St Cuthbert became more and more well known. The shrine of St Cuthbert was visited by hundreds of pilgrims in the same way as pilgrims had visited Lindisfarne in earlier years.

THE CATHEDRAL FROM THE RIVER 1892 30730

The picturesque building seen below the cathedral in this photograph is the old fulling mill, standing beside its weir. Once the property of the Priors of Durham, the fulling mill was once known as the Jesus Mill; it now houses the Durham University Museum of Archaeology. The mill dates from the start of the 15th century, when it played its part in the growing cloth trade of that time. During the 1950s it was a popular riverside café, before being converted into the present-day museum, where exhibits illustrate the early history of Durham and the surrounding areas.

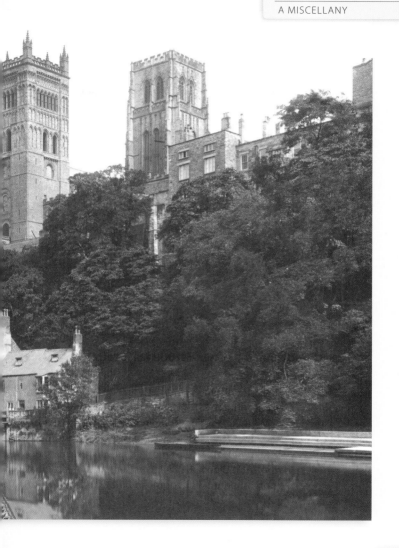

THE CATHEDRAL, THE GALILEE CHAPEL 1892 30753

DURHAM SCHOOL 1929 82407

To the left of photograph 30759, below, is the entrance to the 100ft-long Great Hall of Durham Castle, built during the reign of Bishop Bek. The corner tower houses the Black Staircase (shown on page 47), which when completed in 1662 was free-standing, even though it rises through four floors. In later years the staircase had to be supported with columns owing to a substantial increase in downward weight caused by the building of an additional room on the top storey. The mixture of architectural styles and the work of individual bishops be identified by the coats of arms which are placed in conspicuous places on the walls, including those of Bishop Cosin, Bishop Pudset, Bishop Trevor and Bishop Tunstall.

THE CASTLE 1892 30759

Did You Know?
DURHAM
A MISCELLANY

The grimacing face of the sanctuary knocker seen in photograph
9434, opposite, is hardly a welcoming sight for visitors or those
seeking refuge in the cathedral. It represents the right of sanctuary
for fugitives, who could find temporary shelter in the cathedral from
their pursuers. The right of sanctuary can be traced back to the
year AD597, and later Saxon laws gave these special privileges to St
Cuthbert's Community in around AD900. The Normans continued to
observe the tradition, and at Durham sanctuary was granted for 37
days. The Galilee bell was tolled to inform everyone that a fugitive
was present, and he would only be admitted if he had no weapons.
He would be given food and drink and made to wear a black gown
with a large yellow cross of St Cuthbert on the left shoulder. In fact,
it was not really necessary for the pursued to enter the cathedral,
because the boundaries of sanctuary probably extended as far as
Neville's Cross and Gilesgate. A replica knocker now replaces the
original, which can be seen in the Treasures of St Cuthbert exhibition
in the cathedral.

It seems likely that what later became the Palatinate of Durham
(see page 21) may have had its origins in grants and privileges
that predate the Norman Conquest, those made by King Egfrith
to Cuthbert himself on his elevation to the see of Lindisfarne
in AD685. There also appear to have been further grants of
land by Guthred the Dane and Alfred the Great, and these were
ratified by William the Conqueror.

THE CATHEDRAL, THE NORTH DOOR, THE SANCTUARY KNOCKER c1877 9434

THE CATHEDRAL, THE UNDERCROFT c1862 1119

The strategic importance of Durham became evident after the Norman invasion of England in 1066. The old Saxon defences were replaced, and a more sophisticated stronghold was founded beside the minster in 1072 by orders of William I (the Conqueror). Initially Durham's castle consisted of a timber stockade on an earthen mound, but by the end of the century the stronghold had been fortified and a bailey built around the level ground to the west. Over the years a succession of Prince-Bishops have added important sections to the great building. In the 1930s a huge rescue operation had to be carried out to underpin the subsiding foundations; while the cathedral was built on solid bedrock, the castle was built on less substantial material.

Local tradition says that William I visited Durham with the intention of viewing the uncorrupted body of St Cuthbert. He ordered his men to expose the body, and threatened to put to death all Durham churchmen of senior rank if it were found that the saint's body was not in an incorrupt state. But before the king had even looked at the saint's coffin, he found himself breathless and panic-stricken by a sudden burning fever. Thinking himself to be possessed by some strange force associated with St Cuthbert, he quickly fled from Durham and would not dismount his horse until he had crossed the River Tees into Yorkshire. The lane by which he made his hasty retreat from Durham acquired the name of 'King's Ride', or Kingsgate, which in those days led to a ford across the River Wear. Today it is called Bow Lane, which leads across the River Wear by means of the Kingsgate footbridge.

THE CATHEDRAL FROM OBSERVATORY HILL 1918 68213

Auckland Castle at Bishop Auckland, also known as Auckland Palace, seen in photograph 30706, opposite, began as a manor house built in about 1183 by Bishop Pudsey, but it was later converted into a castle by Bishop Anthony Bek in the 14th century. It has been the home of the Bishops of Durham for over 800 years. Over hundreds of years the castle was expanded until in 1832 it became the official residence of the Bishop of Durham and the administrative centre for the diocese.

Entries in the Sanctuary Book at Durham Cathedral record that between 1464 and 1525 no less than 331 fugitives were admitted, of which 283 were murderers. The custom of the right of sanctuary was recognised throughout the land up to the highest level, and lasted until 1623; failure to observe it might lead to excommunication or death. It was an attempt by the Church to alleviate the severity of the laws of the time, and offer a criminal the chance to repent and atone. The only people who could not claim the right of sanctuary were witches, heretics or those who had committed a crime in church. During the period of sanctuary, the fugitive was expected to be obedient and contrite, confessing his sins, and discuss his case with the Bishop or a priest. At the end of the period, the fugitive would have to decide whether to leave and stand trial, or to plead guilty and 'abjure the realm' - a medieval form of deportation or banishment. An abjurer would usually have to leave the realm from a port some distance away, and would have to make the journey dressed in sackcloth and ashes, barefoot and carrying a cross. If he strayed from the main road he could be executed on the spot.

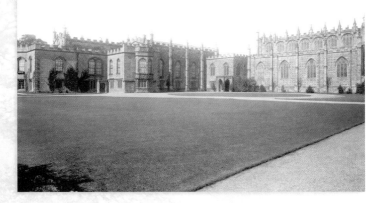

BISHOP AUCKLAND, THE CASTLE 1892 30706

PREBENDS' HOUSE 1914 67128

THE CATHEDRAL, THE NORTH DOOR 1923 74081

The main entrance into the cathedral is the great north door, shown in photograph 74081, opposite, which was made in the 12th century. Bishop Pudsey created the north porch in the 1150s, and it was then that the door's sanctuary knocker was fitted (see photograph 9434 on page 15). There was once a small room above the north porch where two monks would keep vigil day and night, watching for fugitives seeking sanctuary. Note the iron outer gates - these were fitted after it was discovered in 1915 that the northern suffragettes were planning to damage one of the pillars in the nave to gain publicity for the 'Votes for Women' cause. A local suffragette did not support the idea and gave a word of warning, so the iron grille was fitted as a precaution.

Under Norman rule, Durham became an important administrative centre. William the Conqueror granted it the status of a Palatinate, which was ruled over by warrior Prince-Bishops; they were kings in all but name and held ecclesiastical and political sovereignty over the Palatinate of Durham. They had complete control, which meant having their own army, mint and courts, and the right to levy taxes, create barons, grant charters for markets and fairs, and negotiate truces with the Scots. The word 'bishopric' means 'the realm of the bishop', which in those days meant the area between the Rivers Tyne and Tees - this later became known as the County Palatinate of Durham. These lands were intended to act as a buffer zone between England and Scotland; from here the warrior bishops' strong forces could act quickly to quell invaders from the north. The first of the Prince-Bishops was a Norman, Walcher of Lorraine, who succeeded the last Saxon Bishop, Aethelwin. In 1076 Walcher was also created Earl of Northumberland following the execution of the Saxon Earl Waltheof for conspiracy, and for the first time two of the most important and most powerful titles in the north were held by one man.

The first Prince-Bishop of Durham, William Walcher, was murdered at Gateshead in 1081. His replacement was William St Carileph, the man responsible for building the present cathedral, which occupies the site of the old Anglo-Saxon stone minster. Carileph began its construction in 1093. He designed the greater part of the cathedral as it stands today; the new building was completed to the bishop's designs in around 40 years. Unfortunately, Carileph did not live to see the completion of the structure.

Massive columns support the impressive stone-ribbed vaulted roof of the 900-year-old nave of Durham's cathedral, the earliest example of rib vaulting in Europe. This structural innovation was of enormous significance, as it became a widely used feature in later Gothic cathedrals. The magnificent Neville screen seen in photograph 9418, opposite, was a gift from the Neville family in celebration of the victory against the Scots at the Battle of Neville's Cross in 1346. In honour of his victory, Ralph Neville became the first layman to be allowed burial in the cathedral. Behind the screen is the tomb of St Cuthbert. A wooden plaque bears the following inscription: 'Borne by his faithful friends from his loved home on Lindisfarne, here, after long wanderings, rests the body of St Cuthbert in whose honour William of St Carileph built this cathedral church, and at his side lies buried the head of St Oswald King of Northumbria and martyr, slain in battle by the heathen whom he so long defied'.

'I unhesitatingly gave Durham my vote for best cathedral on planet Earth'. (Bill Bryson, 'Notes From A Small Island', 1995)

FRAMWELLGATE BRIDGE AND THE CASTLE 1892 30739

THE CASTLE 1892 30761

The relationship between England, Scotland and the Palatinate of Durham was a little fluid at certain times in history. During the reign of David I of Scotland, the peace treaty following the Battle of the Standard (1138) had resulted in David's son Henry being granted the earldom of Northumbria, but without any claim to the territory of St Cuthbert. Later, Henry II of England insisted that Northumbria be returned; Hugh le Puiset, who was created Bishop of Durham in 1153, entered into a secret treaty with William, the Lion of Scotland, in 1173, and William the Lion launched an invasion aided by le Puiset. The Scots were granted the fortress of Northallerton, an outpost of the Palatinate in Yorkshire, and free passage for their troops. French and Flemish allies of the Scots were allowed to use the port of Hartlepool. However, William the Lion was captured at Alnwick and taken to the fortress of Falaise in Normandy; eventually he acknowledged Henry II as his feudal lord. Bishop le Puiset was punished by being heavily fined and having the castles of Durham, Northallerton and Norham temporarily confiscated.

Apart from aiding the Scots, as detailed above, Bishop le Puiset was responsible for some significant contributions to Durham. It was he who was responsible for Elvet Bridge, thereby providing the peninsula with direct road access to the south, and he also founded Sherburn Hospital c1181 for the treatment of lepers. In 1183 le Puiset ordered the equivalent of a Domesday Book survey of the Palatinate to be made. Details relating to the village of Boldon form the first substantial entry, and the survey became known as the Boldon Book.

At the far end of the cathedral choir is the high altar. Above it is the magnificent Rose Window, over 98ft in circumference (see photograph 30745, opposite). It shows Christ, 'the Saviour of the World' as the inscription says, surrounded by the twelve apostles and the twenty-four elders from the Book of Revelation.

Palace Green is a large, well-tended area between the castle and the cathedral, enclosed on both sides by a range of historic buildings dating from the 18th century. Most of these now belong to Durham University, and include the former Grammar School, located near the cathedral towers. The great space of Palace Green was created by Bishop Flambard at the beginning of the 12th century, when he decided to demolish the existing clutter of wooden houses and the market place because of the potential fire hazard to the castle and the cathedral.

Not all visitors to Durham have been impressed by the city; Daniel Defoe said in 1724: 'The city of Durham appears like a confused heap of stone and brick, accumulated so as to cover a mountain, round which a river winds its brawling course. The streets are generally narrow, dark and unpleasant, and many of them impassable in consequence of their declivity'.

Elvet Bridge, which was built by Bishop Hugh le Puiset in 1160 to give the peninsula direct road access to the south, was repaired by Bishop Richard Fox between 1494 and 1501. During the floods of 1771 the bridge was badly damaged, and in 1804-05 the opportunity was taken to widen it. However, it still incorporates some original 12th-century stonework.

THE CATHEDRAL, THE CHOIR, LOOKING EAST 1892 30745

ELVET BRIDGE 1918 68235

Though called the Count's House, the building shown in photograph 67129, opposite, is in fact a folly, dating from about 1820. The original Count's House was about 100 yards nearer to Prebends' Bridge, and was the home of Count Joseph Boruwlaski, a Polish dwarf who stood just 39 inches high. Often referred to as the Polish Dwarf, the Little Count or 'Lord' Tom Thumb, he was an accomplished violinist whose musical talent earned him many notable admirers, including George IV and Marie Antoinette. He died at the grand old age of 97, and having established himself as a respected member of Durham society was buried in the cathedral. Sad to say, the real Count's House is today just a neglected ruin; its association with a diminutive man who figured larger than life in the city's history is now apparently forgotten, although there is a statue of Boruwlaski in the Town Hall.

The area of Old Elvet was once the site of the city's horse fair. On the right of photograph 67127, opposite, is the well-known hotel, the Royal County, created in the 19th century out of former town houses belonging to the Ratcliffe and Bowes families. Inside, the hotel is notable for its impressive black staircase dating from 1660, which is said to have been brought here from Loch Leven Castle in Scotland. The cast-iron balconies such as that on the hotel were a feature of town houses in Durham belonging to wealthy families. The balcony at No 30 is of particular interest: it afforded the occupants the very best of views of the public hangings that used to take place on Court Green.

THE COUNT'S HOUSE 1914 67129

OLD ELVET 1914 67127

ST MARY THE LESS CHURCH 1918 68227

The Church of St Mary the Less was originally one of the smallest parish churches in England, and was built in the 12th century by one of the mighty Nevilles of Brancepeth Castle (see photograph 68227, opposite). The church was built as a place of worship for the retainers and fighting men who came to staff the city walls; since 1919 it has been the college chapel for St John's, one of the smallest university colleges. In the church is a memorial to Count Joseph Boruwlaski, the Polish dwarf (see page 29). Although he was buried in the cathedral, his memorial was erected here because the wording on it was considered to be inappropriate to the cathedral: 'Count Joseph Boruwlaski of Poland, who measured no more than three feet and three inches'. His burial site in the cathedral is marked instead by the simple letters 'JB'.

The work of building Durham Cathedral can be attributed to several distinct periods. The nave, transepts and the four west choir bays were built to Bishop Carileph's design, between 1093 and 1133. Bishop Hugh le Puiset (who was known more affectionately as Bishop Pudsey) added the Galilee Chapel at the western end in 1175; the two west towers were built between 1217 and 1226; then the east end of the choir was altered and the Chapel of the Nine Altars erected between 1242 and 1280. The great central tower was rebuilt between 1465 and 1495 after lightning and fire destroyed its predecessor some 60 years earlier.

The atmospheric vaulted undercroft is the oldest part of the cathedral, and is now used to house the Treasures of St Cuthbert exhibition. One of the exhibits is the embroidered Anglo-Saxon stole that came from St Cuthbert's coffin.

THE SHIRE HALL 1921 70730

Built of red brick, the Shire Hall was designed by local
architects H Barnes and F E Coates, and was completed in 1898
(photograph 70730, above). After the authorities moved out
in 1963 the Hall went on to enjoy a new lease of life as the
administrative headquarters for Durham University.

Built between 1772 and 1778, the three-arched Prebends' Bridge
replaced a mid 16th-century footbridge that had been washed away
during the floods of 1771 (see photograph 30756 on page 34). It was
designed by George Nicholson, architect to the Dean and Chapter
of Durham Cathedral. The bridge is so named because only the
prebends or canons of the cathedral have the right to drive a vehicle
across it.

Framwellgate Bridge was the scene of a murder in 1318, when the Bishop of Durham's steward, Richard Fitzmarmaduke, was killed by his cousin Ralph Neville, nicknamed 'the Peacock of the North', after a longstanding feud between the two men.

The famous Roman Catholic seminary of Ushaw College at Ushaw Moor is the main centre in the north of England for the training of Roman Catholic priests. Its establishment dates back to the foundation of the great seminary at Douai in France, which was founded in 1568 to supply Catholic missionaries to England during a period of Catholic repression. The college is the home of St Cuthbert's finger ring, which may be worn by the Roman Catholic Bishop of Hexham and Newcastle on special occasions.

USHAW MOOR, USHAW COLLEGE c1960 U17009

THE CATHEDRAL 1892 30741

PREBENDS' BRIDGE 1892 30756

Dedicated to Our Lord and St Mary the Virgin, Durham Cathedral is considered to be the finest Romanesque church in Europe. From whatever direction the city is approached, this towering structure dominates the landscape. The sheer size of the cathedral is awesome: the central tower soars to a phenomenal 281ft and has 325 steps, should we wish to tackle the ascent. The entire building stretches 470ft from the east wall of the Chapel of Nine Altars to the west wall of the Galilee Chapel, and the great nave runs for 201ft, its roof vault rising some 72ft.

The long, battlemented single-storey stone building immediately in front of the west towers of the cathedral (shown in photograph 30730 on pages 10-11) is the Galilee Chapel, which is also the cathedral's Lady Chapel, dating from 1175. Bishop Hugh le Puiset had attempted to build a Lady Chapel at the east end, the usual place for the Lady Chapel in cathedrals, but construction was plagued with problems, including insecure foundations and cracking walls. These events were interpreted as a sign that Durham's saintly misogynist was angry at the thought of women being allowed so close to his tomb, so the chapel was constructed at the west end. However, at a later stage another chapel, the Chapel of the Nine Altars, was built at the cathedral's east end - mysteriously, this seems to have been built without any problems.

The cathedral library is housed in the former monks' dormitory above the western walkway of the cloisters. It dates from the 14th century, and has an impressive roof of oak beams, which looks like the hull of an upturned ship. The library now belongs to the Dean and chapter, and houses a collection of Anglo-Saxon and Viking crosses from throughout the ancient kingdom of Northumbria.

THE VIEW FROM THE RAILWAY STATION 1892 30728

Photograph 30728, above, shows a train belonging to the North Eastern Railway just about to ease out on to the great viaduct, built by Robert Stephenson in 1857, that carries the line 100ft above the streets of Durham. The North Eastern had two stations serving Durham. Elvet closed in 1931 to passenger traffic, but remained open for goods until January 1954. Gilesgate closed to passengers in April 1857 but survived for goods traffic until November 1966.

Organ building was an important Durham industry in the 19th century, and the firm Harrison & Harrison, founded in 1861 and one of the most famous organ builders in Britain, still exists today. The company's work included the organs for many cathedrals, including Ely, Winchester, Worcester, and Durham itself. Other notable organs made by the firm include those at Westminster Abbey, York Minster and the Royal Albert Hall.

The old Town Hall, known as the Guildhall, was built in 1356, and many alterations were made right up to the middle of the 18th century. The Guildhall has connections with the old city guilds, some of which still exist and meet here. The main function of the medieval guilds was to oversee and guarantee high standards of workmanship and to ensure a monopoly for their members. By the middle of the 19th century the Guildhall had ceased to be a suitable building to accommodate the business of the growing city, so in 1850 a new town hall was built behind the old structure. The new hall was designed to be a smaller-scale version of Westminster Hall - photograph 68231, below, shows the impressive hammer-beam roof. Other interesting features include superb stained-glass windows, paintings and heraldic symbols, and a magnificent fireplace made of local Prudhoe stone.

THE TOWN HALL, THE INTERIOR 1918 68231

The Galilee Chapel of the cathedral is also the Lady Chapel, once the only part of the cathedral that could be entered by women, according to the rules of the Benedictine order of monks. In the Galilee Chapel is the black, marble topped tomb of the scholar and historian known as the Venerable Bede, the Jarrow monk who wrote 79 books, the most famous of which is his 'Ecclesiastical History of the English People', one of the main, and most reliable, sources for the history of the Anglo-Saxon period. Bede wrote in both Latin and Anglo-Saxon, and his scholarship brought him international recognition. Bede died in AD735 aged 62, having just completed a translation into Anglo-Saxon of St John's Gospel. He was buried at Jarrow in a special porch on the side of the monastery church, but his remains were later interred under the high altar of the church. In the 11th century his remains were stolen from Jarrow and brought to Durham by the cathedral's sacrist. Most of what we know about St Cuthbert comes from Bede's 'Life of St Cuthbert'.

One of the colourful bishops in Durham's story was Anthony Bek, who reigned between 1284 and 1310. He was also Lord of Man, Patriarch of Jerusalem and a talented soldier. He was a contemporary of Edward I, 'Longshanks', one of the most ruthless and able kings ever to rule England. In 1296, Bishop Bek actively supported Edward when he stripped John Baliol of the Scottish throne for failing to attend the parliament at Newcastle. Two years later, Bek commanded a wing of the English army at the Battle of Falkirk; yet he opposed the right of visitation claimed by the Archbishops of York, and supported the Nevilles when they contested Edward's right to call on Palatinate troops for service beyond its borders.

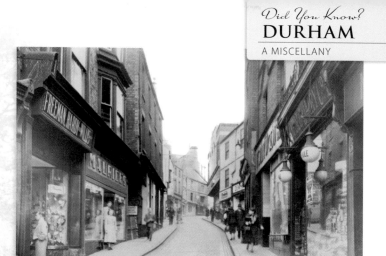

SILVER STREET c1955 D71024

THE RIVER AND THE RACECOURSE 1918 68232

NORTH ROAD c1955 D71059

THE CASTLE 1921 70724

Framwellgate was Durham's first bridge over the Wear. The original bridge was built by Bishop Flambard in the 1120s, when dwellings between the castle and the cathedral were cleared to create Palace Green, and the townsfolk who lived there were relocated to Crossgate. The bridge was rebuilt at the beginning of the 15th century after being damaged by flooding. The peninsula end was once defended by a gatehouse, but this fortification was demolished in 1760. The bridge was widened in 1856, and until the 1970s all city centre traffic came into Durham over this bridge and through the narrow Silver Street.

At the west end of Prebends' Bridge is a plaque featuring an extract from Sir Walter Scott's poem on Durham:

'Grey towers of Durham, yet well I love thy mixed and varied piles,
Half church of God, half castle 'gainst the Scot,
And long to roam these venerable aisles
With records stored of deeds long since forgot'.

The original choir stalls and font canopy of the cathedral were burnt by the Scots prisoners who were incarcerated in the cathedral after the Battle of Dunbar in 1650. A new font canopy (as well as new choir stalls and a richly carved wooden screen dividing the nave from the choir) was designed for Bishop Cosin by James Clement, a Durham architect, and installed in 1663. The ornate decoration of the octagonal canopy emphasises the significance of baptism in the life of the Church. The huge marble font used today also dates from the time of James Cosin, who was a canon at Durham during the reign of Charles I, and later Bishop of Durham under Charles II.

41

The Memorial Chapel in the cathedral was dedicated in 1924 to commemorate Durham's own regiment, the Durham Light Infantry. It contains the regimental colours and books of remembrance listing the names of those who fell in battle.

A university was officially established at Durham in 1657 during the Commonwealth, but it was suppressed following the Restoration. Durham was finally granted its university in 1832. In 1835 Bishop van Mildbert exercised one of his few remaining powers as a Prince-Bishop by turning over the castle to the university, and the keep was reconstructed in 1840 to provide student accommodation.

Although coalmines are now almost non-existent in County Durham, one of the biggest events in the county nowadays is the Miners' Gala, held in Durham in July. The event is now but a shadow of its former self, but for decades it was the focal point of the year for every miner and his family. At its height, in the years prior to the First World War, the event was the largest annual gathering by the working classes in Britain, with crowds often in excess of 100,000. During the 1925 Gala, the year before the General Strike, the Dean of Durham was thrown into the River Wear by miners who had mistaken him for the bishop, who had unwisely expressed the view that miners did not deserve an increase in pay. Many great speakers from the Labour movement attended the Gala, including Clement Atlee, Ernest Bevin, Aneurin Bevan, Harold Wilson, Michael Foot and Tony Benn. Although still recognised as one of the last great miners' gatherings, the Durham Miners' Gala today is more of a festival with a varied programme of entertainment.

Photograph D71301, below, shows the Market Place, dominated by St Nicholas's Church. In 1857 this Victorian church replaced an earlier church of St Nicholas, which dated from the 12th century. On the left of the photograph, next to the Prudential Assurance building, is the Market Tavern, where the Miners' Union was formed in 1871. In the foreground is the statue of Neptune on top of the ocatagonal pant (a northern word for a public fountain). Neptune was placed here in 1729 to symbolise an ambitious plan to turn Durham into an inland sea port; this would have resulted in the unthinkable - the joining of the Rivers Tyne and Wear! The pant was demolished in 1923, and Neptune was moved to a life of solitude in Wharton Park. Fortunately he was returned to his rightful place in the Market Square in 1991. Neptune's neighbour in the photograph is the equestrian statue of the 3rd Marquess of Londonderry, one of the Duke of Wellington's cavalry generals, who owned collieries around Durham and also constructed Seaham Harbour in 1828. The statue was sculpted by Raphael Monti, but the commission bankrupted him.

MARKET PLACE c1915 D71301

ST CUTHBERT'S CHURCH c1883 16160

SPORTING DURHAM

Durham City Rowing Regatta was founded in 1834. Professional races were held between 1834 and 1947, and amateur events have been held since then. In the 19th century professional rowing was a huge spectator sport, and the top rowers competed around the world for big prizes and were the sporting celebrities of those times. During this era the regatta attracted the most famous rowers of their day. James Renworth, Harry Clasper and Robert Chambers, who all rowed at the regatta, were internationally renowned.

Durham FC has had an interesting and varied history since its formation in 1918. In its early days the club had a brief spell in the Football League. The club has been disbanded twice and has existed in its current format since 1950. The club played at four different grounds before moving to its new home at Ferens Park. One of the club's best-known players was Sammy Crooks, who only played for one season during Durham's period in the Football League, but later went on to play for England 26 times, whilst a Derby County player.

Perhaps the most famous and successful Durham-born footballer was George Camsell (1902-1966). He was born in Framwellgate Moor, and played for Durham for several years before signing for Middlesbrough. He scored 59 goals for the club in one season, 1926-27, the second highest ever achieved. He scored a total of 345 goals in 453 games for Middlesbrough, and is the fifth highest goal scorer in English League Football. George Camsell was capped for England 9 times and scored 18 goals for his country, including four in one game against Spain in 1929.

QUIZ QUESTIONS

Answers on page 50.

1. What is the 'death chair', and where can you find it?

2. What was the gruesome work for which four Durham women each received a cow in payment in the 11th century?

3. How did Silver Street get its name?

4. A little way inside the main cathedral building there is a line of black marble in the cathedral floor - what is the reason for this?

5. What is special about the Bishop's Throne in the cathedral, and what is the reputed reason for this?

6. A tomb in Durham Cathedral houses the remains of the person who was responsible for devising our dating system - who was this?

7. Why is there a carving of a milkmaid and a cow on the north wall of Durham Cathedral?

8. A particularly unusual apron is held in the collection of the Oriental Museum at the Department of East Asian Studies, Durham University - what is it?

9. Which king walked six miles barefoot from Garmondsway (now a deserted medieval village situated near Coxhoe) to Durham, to visit the shrine of St Cuthbert?

10. When and where was the Battle of Neville's Cross, and who fought it?

RECIPE

BACON FLODDIES

Bacon Floddies are a traditional dish from the north of England. They can be eaten on their own, but are usually served with sausages or bacon and eggs for breakfast or supper.

Ingredients

225g/8oz peeled potatoes
2 medium onions, peeled
175g/6oz bacon rashers, finely chopped
50g/2oz self-raising flour

Salt and freshly ground black pepper
2 eggs, beaten
4 tablespoonfuls bacon dripping or oil

Grate the potatoes and onion into a mixing bowl. Add the finely chopped bacon, the flour and the seasoning and mix well. Add the beaten eggs, mixing them well through all the ingredients. Heat the dripping or oil in a heavy pan until hot but not smoking. Add tablespoonfuls of the floddies to the pan, not overcrowding them, and fry carefully on both sides until they are golden and cooked through. Drain on paper towels and keep hot in a dish until ready to serve.

RECIPE

DURHAM PIKELETS

Ingredients

225g/8oz self-raising flour
1 teaspoonful bicarbonate of soda
1 teaspoonful cream of tartar

40g/1½oz margarine
40g/1½oz sugar
300ml/½ pint (approx) buttermilk or low-fat milk
½ teaspoonful salt

Sift the flour, soda, cream of tartar and salt together into a bowl, then rub in the margarine until the mixture resembles fine breadcrumbs, and mix in the sugar. Make a well in the centre of the mixture and add enough buttermilk or milk, beating lightly, to give a dropping consistency. Drop the mixture in spoonfuls onto a hot, well-greased griddle or heavy frying pan, and cook the pikelets for about 4 minutes on each side until they are golden brown. Serve hot, spread with plenty of butter, and jam if liked.

QUIZ ANSWERS

1. On display at the Heritage Centre in the Church of St Mary-le-Bow is the 'death chair', a sedan chair given by Durham School, where it was used in the 19th century to carry sick boys to the sanatorium. It became known by the schoolboys as the 'death chair' because boys ill enough to be carried in it rarely returned.

2. In 1006 Durham was attacked by the Scots; they were quickly repelled, and many of the invaders quite literally lost their heads to an English army comprised of Northumbrians and Yorkshiremen. The Scottish heads were displayed around Durham's walls as a menacing warning against future attacks. Four of the city's women were each presented with the generous gift of a cow for washing the heads and combing the hair of the best-looking Scottish heads on display.

3. The narrow medieval Silver Street is said to have acquired its name from once being the site of a mint where unique Durham coins were produced.

4. At one time, the Lady Chapel (also known as the Galilee Chapel at Durham) was the only part of the cathedral which women were allowed to enter. The black marble line in the floor marked the point beyond which women were not allowed to go.

5. The impressive Bishop's Throne is said to be the highest in Christendom. Below the throne is the tomb of Bishop Thomas Hatfield, who is reputed to have decided that the Bishop of Durham deserved a throne at least equal in height to that of the Bishop of Rome - the Pope.

6. The monk known to history as the Venerable Bede (AD673-735), whose remains were brought from Jarrow to lie in a tomb in the Galilee Chapel (see page 38). Bede was a scholar and historian, and devised the AD and BC dating system for dates before and after the birth of Christ.

7. The 18th-century carving of a milkmaid and a cow on the north wall of the cathedral recalls the legend of how Durham was first discovered by the monks seeking a resting place for the remains of St Cuthbert - see page 9.

8. The Oriental Museum at the Department of East Asian Studies, Durham University holds a unique collection of oriental art and archaeology. Amongst the items on display are carvings from Japan and China, Assyrian reliefs, artefacts from ancient Egypt, Indian paintings and teak panels from a Burmese palace, but the most gruesome (and fascinating) item is probably the Tibetan magician's apron that is made from human bones.

9. King Canute, in 1027. He made the barefoot journey as a mark of respect to St Cuthbert.

10. The Battle of Neville's Cross was fought in 1346, just outside Durham, between Scottish forces and an English army raised by Edward III's wife, Queen Philippa. On the western outskirts of the city a cross marks the position of the left flank of the English forces who defeated the Scots and captured David II. One of the commanders of the victorious English army was Ralph Neville of Raby Castle, 16 miles south-west of Durham, who became the first layman to be buried in the cathedral after his death in 1367.

FRANCIS FRITH

PIONEER VICTORIAN PHOTOGRAPHER

Francis Frith, founder of the world-famous photographic archive, was a complex and multi-talented man. A devout Quaker and a highly successful Victorian businessman, he was philosophical by nature and pioneering in outlook. By 1855 he had already established a wholesale grocery business in Liverpool, and sold it for the astonishing sum of £200,000, which is the equivalent today of over £15,000,000. Now in his thirties, and captivated by the new science of photography, Frith set out on a series of pioneering journeys up the Nile and to the Near East.

INTRIGUE AND EXPLORATION

He was the first photographer to venture beyond the sixth cataract of the Nile. Africa was still the mysterious 'Dark Continent', and Stanley and Livingstone's historic meeting was a decade into the future. The conditions for picture taking confound belief. He laboured for hours in his wicker dark-room in the sweltering heat of the desert, while the volatile chemicals fizzed dangerously in their trays. Back in London he exhibited his photographs and was 'rapturously cheered' by members of the Royal Society. His reputation as a photographer was made overnight.

VENTURE OF A LIFE-TIME

By the 1870s the railways had threaded their way across the country, and Bank Holidays and half-day Saturdays had been made obligatory by Act of Parliament. All of a sudden the working man and his family were able to enjoy days out, take holidays, and see a little more of the world.

With typical business acumen, Francis Frith foresaw that these new tourists would enjoy having souvenirs to commemorate their days out. For the next thirty years he travelled the country by train and by pony and trap, producing fine photographs of seaside resorts and beauty spots that were keenly bought by millions of Victorians. These prints were painstakingly pasted into family albums and pored over during the dark nights of winter, rekindling precious memories of summer excursions. Frith's studio was soon supplying retail shops all over the country, and by 1890 F Frith & Co had become the greatest specialist photographic publishing company in the world, with over 2,000 sales outlets, and pioneered the picture postcard.

FRANCIS FRITH'S LEGACY

Francis Frith had died in 1898 at his villa in Cannes, his great project still growing. By 1970 the archive he created contained over a third of a million pictures showing 7,000 British towns and villages.

Frith's legacy to us today is of immense significance and value, for the magnificent archive of evocative photographs he created provides a unique record of change in the cities, towns and villages throughout Britain over a century and more. Frith and his fellow studio photographers revisited locations many times down the years to update their views, compiling for us an enthralling and colourful pageant of British life and character.

We are fortunate that Frith was dedicated to recording the minutiae of everyday life. For it is this sheer wealth of visual data, the painstaking chronicle of changes in dress, transport, street layouts, buildings, housing and landscape that captivates us so much today, offering us a powerful link with the past and with the lives of our ancestors.

Computers have now made it possible for Frith's many thousands of images to be accessed almost instantly. The archive offers every one of us an opportunity to examine the places where we and our families have lived and worked down the years. Its images, depicting our shared past, are now bringing pleasure and enlightenment to millions around the world a century and more after his death.

For further information visit: www.francisfrith.com

INTERIOR DECORATION

Frith's photographs can be seen framed and as giant wall murals in thousands of pubs, restaurants, hotels, banks, retail stores and other public buildings throughout Britain. These provide interesting and attractive décor, generating strong local interest and acting as a powerful reminder of gentler days in our increasingly busy and frenetic world.

FRITH PRODUCTS

All Frith photographs are available as prints and posters in a variety of different sizes and styles. In the UK we also offer a range of other gift and stationery products illustrated with Frith photographs, although many of these are not available for delivery outside the UK – see our web site for more information on the products available for delivery in your country.

THE INTERNET

Over 100,000 photographs of Britain can be viewed and purchased on the Frith web site. The web site also includes memories and reminiscences contributed by our customers, who have personal knowledge of localities and of the people and properties depicted in Frith photographs. If you wish to learn more about a specific town or village you may find these reminiscences fascinating to browse. Why not add your own comments if you think they would be of interest to others? See **www.francisfrith.com**

PLEASE HELP US BRING FRITH'S PHOTOGRAPHS TO LIFE

Our authors do their best to recount the history of the places they write about. They give insights into how particular towns and villages developed, they describe the architecture of streets and buildings, and they discuss the lives of famous people who lived there. But however knowledgeable our authors are, the story they tell is necessarily incomplete.

Frith's photographs are so much more than plain historical documents. They are living proofs of the flow of human life down the generations. They show real people at real moments in history; and each of those people is the son or daughter of someone, the brother or sister, aunt or uncle, grandfather or grandmother of someone else. All of them lived, worked and played in the streets depicted in Frith's photographs.

We would be grateful if you would give us your insights into the places shown in our photographs: the streets and buildings, the shops, businesses and industries. Post your memories of life in those streets on the Frith website: what it was like growing up there, who ran the local shop and what shopping was like years ago; if your workplace is shown tell us about your working day and what the building is used for now. Read other visitors' memories and reconnect with your shared local history and heritage. With your help more and more Frith photographs can be brought to life, and vital memories preserved for posterity, and for the benefit of historians in the future.

Wherever possible, we will try to include some of your comments in future editions of our books. Moreover, if you spot errors in dates, titles or other facts, please let us know, because our archive records are not always completely accurate—they rely on 140 years of human endeavour and hand-compiled records. You can email us using the contact form on the website.

Thank you!

For further information, trade, or author enquiries
please contact us at the address below:

The Francis Frith Collection, Frith's Barn, Teffont, Salisbury, Wiltshire, England SP3 5QP.
Tel: +44 (0)1722 716 376 Fax: +44 (0)1722 716 881
e-mail: sales@francisfrith.co.uk **www.francisfrith.com**